SPOOKY SITES

LINCOLN PARK ZOO

THOMAS KINGSLEY TROUPE

A Shark Book
SEAHORSE PUBLISHING

Teaching Tips for Caregivers:

You can help your child learn by encouraging them to read widely, both as a leisure activity and as a way of satisfying their curiosity about the world. Reading helps build a strong foundation in language and literacy skills that will help your child succeed in school. This high-interest book will appeal to all readers in intermediate and middle school grades.

Use the following suggestions to help your child grow as a reader.

- Encourage them to read independently at home.
- Encourage them to practice reading aloud.
- Encourage activities that require reading.
- Establish a regular reading time.
- Have your child ask and answer questions about what they read.

Teaching Tips for Teachers:

Engage students throughout the reading process by asking questions like these.

Before Reading
- Ask, "What do you already know about this topic?"
- Ask, "What do you want to learn about this topic?"

During Reading
- Ask, "What is the author trying to teach you?"
- Ask, "How is this like something you have read or seen before?"
- Ask, "How do the text features (headings, index, etc.) help you understand the topic?"

After Reading
- Ask, "What interesting or fun fact did you learn?"
- Ask, "What questions do you still have about the topic? How could you find the answers?"

TABLE OF CONTENTS

Don't Feed the Ghosts!..4
The History of Lincoln Park Zoo...6
Morbid Movers..10
Strange Sightings...14
Real or Hoax?...17
Paranormal Proof?..18
Be a Paranormal Investigator!...20
Glossary...22
Index..23
After Reading Questions..23
About the Author...24

Don't Feed the Ghosts!

It's a dark and windy night. Your hair blows wild on top of your head. Your hand shivers as you guide your flashlight around the zoo. Though you're in a well-populated city, you feel more alone than you ever have.

Most of the animals are asleep in their enclosures. The park paths, usually busy with visitors, are empty. There's not another soul in sight. Or is there? You hear a faint whisper in the distance. Near the Lion House, you see the faded image of a woman walking. She stops, looks your way, then disappears. So should you!

The History of Lincoln Park Zoo

Lincoln Park Zoo is a public zoo located in Chicago, Illinois. It was founded in 1868, which makes it the fourth oldest zoo in North America. The zoo covers 35 acres (14 hectares) and is a popular tourist attraction for anyone visiting "The Windy City." Admission is free.

Lincoln Park Zoo is home to over 200 animal species and 1,000 individual animals. It is also rumored to be the home of a large population of **poltergeists**! Many people have reported having **paranormal** encounters while visiting the zoo.

The zoo is part of the larger Lincoln Park, which many people believe is haunted. A section of the park was once the site of the Chicago City Cemetery. At one time, many of the city's dead were buried there. The first burials were in 1843. Over time, tens of thousands of people were laid to rest in the graveyard.

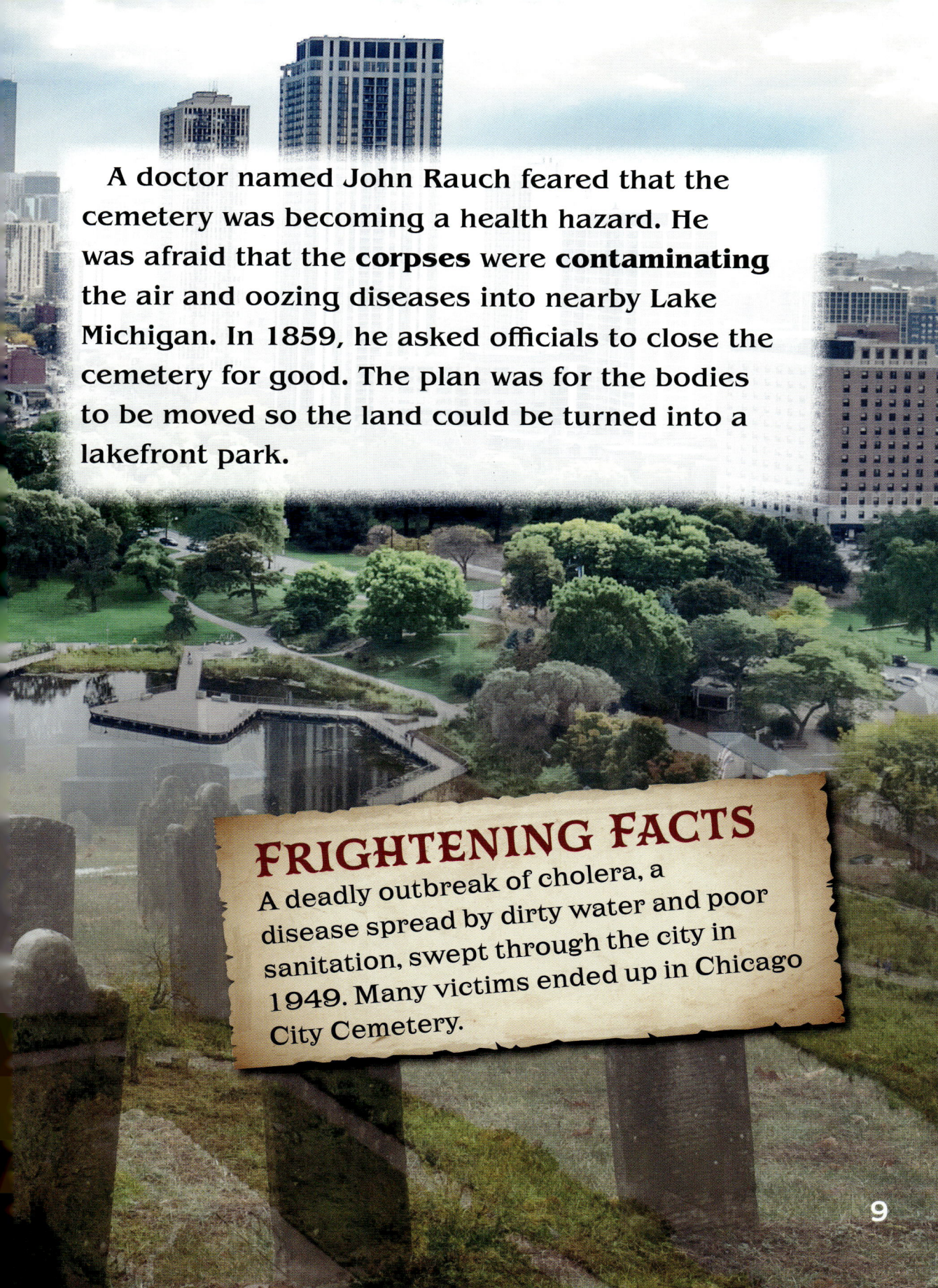

A doctor named John Rauch feared that the cemetery was becoming a health hazard. He was afraid that the **corpses** were **contaminating** the air and oozing diseases into nearby Lake Michigan. In 1859, he asked officials to close the cemetery for good. The plan was for the bodies to be moved so the land could be turned into a lakefront park.

FRIGHTENING FACTS

A deadly outbreak of cholera, a disease spread by dirty water and poor sanitation, swept through the city in 1949. Many victims ended up in Chicago City Cemetery.

Morbid Movers

By 1864, the city ordered burials to stop in Chicago City Cemetery. Despite the order, bodies continued to be **interred** there. In the early 1870s, the decision was made to dig up and move all the bodies. Then, in 1871, the job of relocating the dead became a lot more complicated.

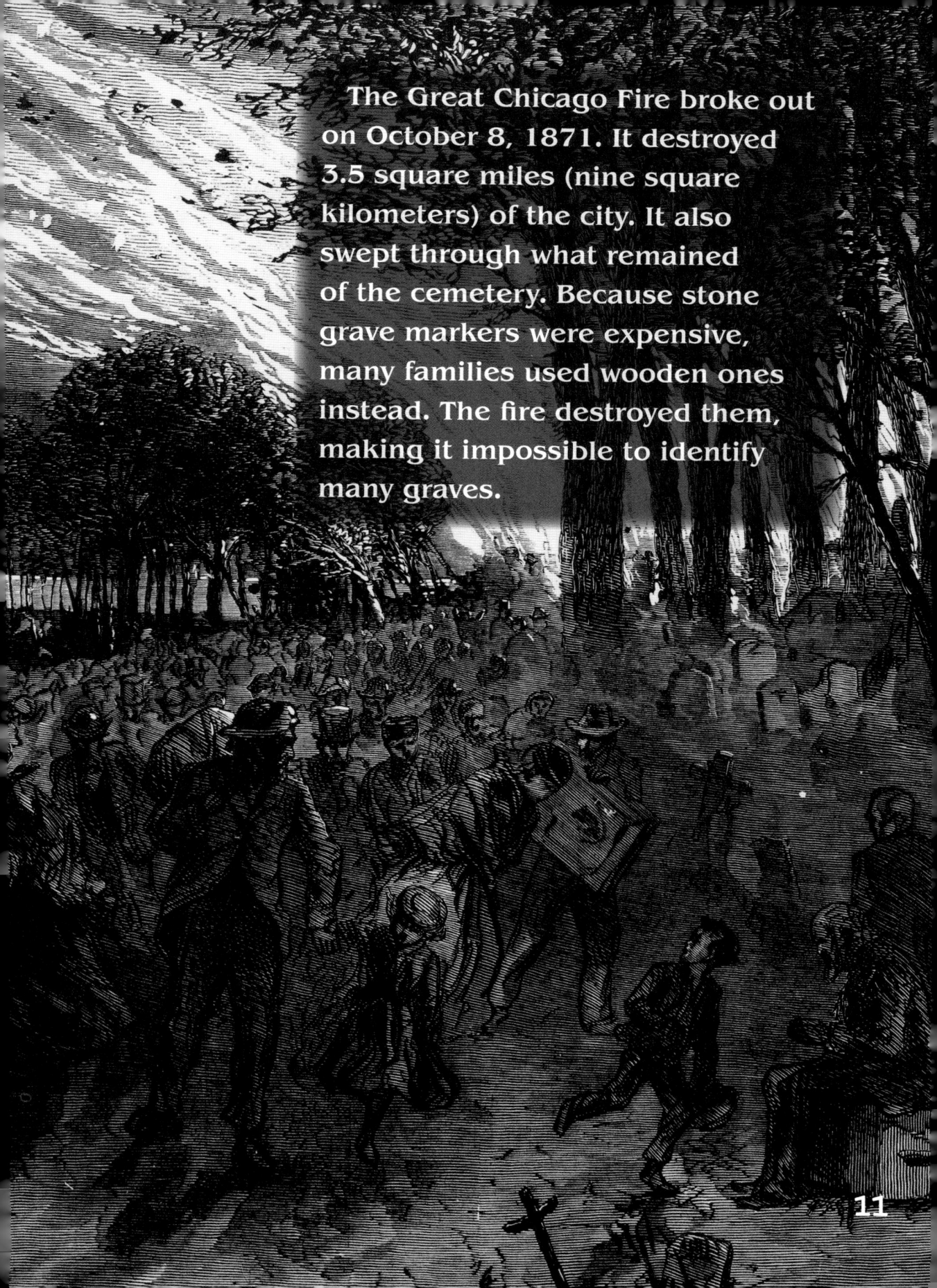

The Great Chicago Fire broke out on October 8, 1871. It destroyed 3.5 square miles (nine square kilometers) of the city. It also swept through what remained of the cemetery. Because stone grave markers were expensive, many families used wooden ones instead. The fire destroyed them, making it impossible to identify many graves.

After the fire, headstones and **vaults** were moved to nearby land set aside for the transferred bodies. It was a **morbid** and horrible job. Bodies were hauled out at a rate of 20 per day. Even so, it took a long time. In 1872, a Chicago newspaper headline read *The Remains of Over 10,000 Dead Persons Still to Be Taken Away.*

FRIGHTENING FACTS

Hundreds of bodies were buried illegally in the Chicago City Cemetery in unmarked graves. Gravediggers would sometimes dig a plot for a newly deceased person only to find another body already there!

Eventually, approximately 22,500 bodies were removed. But there are likely 12,000 bodies still buried beneath Lincoln Park.

Strange Sightings

Some people who visit Lincoln Park Zoo today claim to see ghostly figures. The women's restroom in the basement of the Lion House is rumored to be haunted. The restroom's mirrors are said to reflect men and women dressed in **Victorian** clothing.

FRIGHTENING FACTS

An old bridge near the zoo was known as "suicide bridge." At least 100 people died there by jumping off or falling off the bridge into the lagoon below. The bridge was dismantled in 1919.

Since the bathroom is located below ground, it's possible that the space was once part of a grave. Outside the Lion House, people have reported seeing the **apparition** of a woman wandering near the building.

Visitors have heard otherworldly voices at the zoo. Some of the voices demand, "GET OUT!"

Real or Hoax?

Many graves and tombs were relocated from the site of the Chicago City Cemetery. But one stone structure still stands there, just south of the zoo. It is a **mausoleum** with the family name COUCH carved above its door. The city determined it would be too expensive to move it.

Locals say that if you stand before the mausoleum at midnight, you can visit the **supernatural.** You have to look at the name COUCH and whisper three times, "The graves belong to the dead, not the living." Legend says that the door will then open, revealing a large white ghost who greets visitors. Could this story be true, or is it just a **hoax?**

Paranormal Proof?

For years, paranormal investigators have looked for evidence of ghosts in Lincoln Park. They want to prove that the beloved city zoo and the surrounding park are truly haunted. They try to photograph the old-fashioned ghosts when they appear. Digital audio recorders are used to capture EVP, or electronic voice phenomena. With this method, investigators can record words and phrases from the dead.

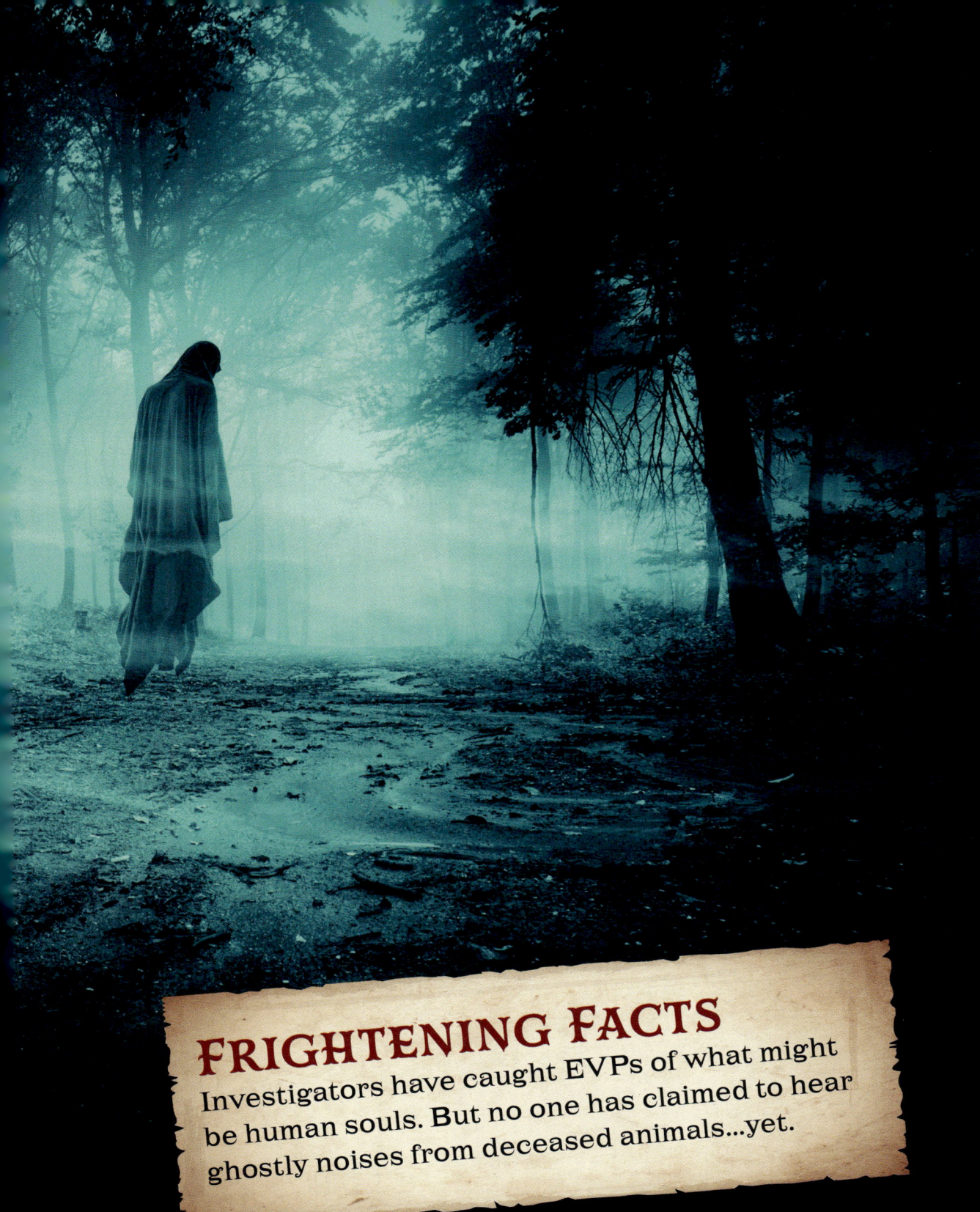

FRIGHTENING FACTS
Investigators have caught EVPs of what might be human souls. But no one has claimed to hear ghostly noises from deceased animals...yet.

Be a Paranormal Investigator!

Whether it's really haunted or not, the Lincoln Park Zoo is a creepy place for the curious to explore. Is it full of the displaced dead looking for their graves? Is the restroom of the Lion House truly a haunted hotspot? No one knows for sure. But one thing is certain: The dark history of Lincoln Park and Lincoln Park Zoo is full of frights!

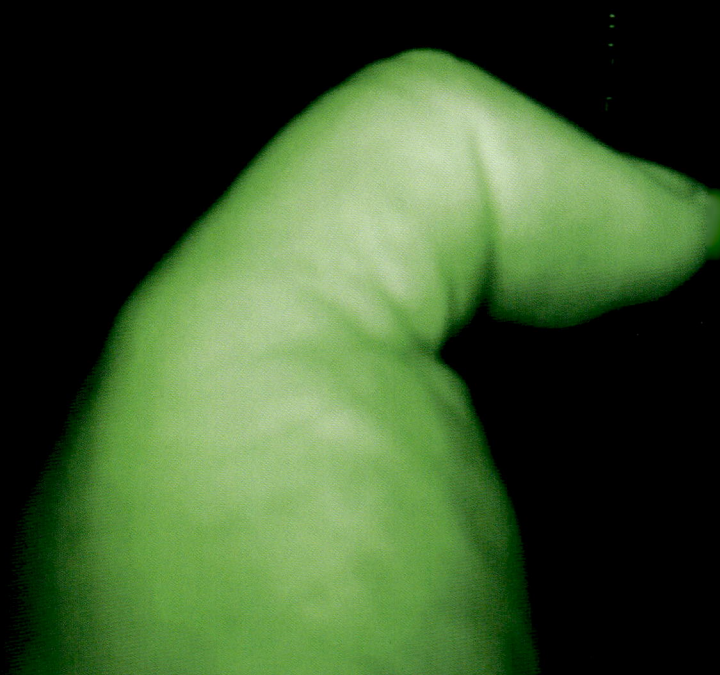

Do you want to be a paranormal investigator? You can! All you really need is a flashlight, an audio recorder, and some bravery. Go to a dark, creepy place. Look around and ask questions. Record the whole EVP session. When you play the recording back, you might hear strange things. Is it something paranormal trying to talk to you? It could be!

Glossary

apparition (ap-puh-RI-shuhn): the supernatural appearance of a person or thing; a ghost or specter

contaminating (kuhn-TAM-uh-nay-ting): making dangerous, dirty, or impure by adding something harmful

corpses (CORPS-is): dead bodies

hoax (hohks): a trick that makes people believe something that is not true

interred (in-TURD): deposited a dead body in the ground or in a tomb

mausoleum (mah-zuh-LEE-uhm): an aboveground building used to store the remains of people who have died

morbid (MOR-bid): gruesome, unpleasant, or related to death

paranormal (pair-uh-NOR-muhl): something that cannot be explained by science

poltergeists (POHL-tur-gysts): ghosts

supernatural (soo-pur-NACH-ur-uhl): existing outside of human experience or knowledge

vaults (vawltz): underground burial chambers

Victorian (vik-TOR-ee-uhn): related to the rule of Queen Victoria in England in the mid- to late-1800s; a time when people wore corsets, bonnets, top hats, bustles, and petticoats

Index

Chicago City Cemetery 8–10, 13, 17

cholera 9

corpses 9

evidence 18

EVP(s) 18, 19, 21

ghost(ly/s) 4, 14, 17-19

Great Chicago Fire 11

haunted 8, 14, 18, 20

investigator(s) 18–21

Lion House 4, 14, 15, 20

mausoleum 17

Rauch, John 9

After Reading Questions

1. What paranormal encounters have people had at Lincoln Park Zoo?

2. Why was the Chicago City Cemetery closed?

3. What complicated efforts to move bodies away from the old cemetery?

4. Do you believe Lincoln Park Zoo is haunted? Why or why not?

About the Author

Thomas Kingsley Troupe is the author of over 200 books for young readers. When he's not writing, he enjoys reading, playing video games, and investigating haunted places with the Twin Cities Paranormal Society. Otherwise, he's probably taking a nap or something. Thomas lives in Woodbury, Minnesota, with his two sons.

Written by: Thomas Kingsley Troupe
Design by: Under the Oaks Media
Editor: Kim Thompson

Photo credits: John Frost Newspapers / Alamy Stock Photo: p. 10-11; Niday Picture Library / Alamy Stock Photo: p. 15; All other images by Shutterstock or in the public domain.

Library of Congress PCN Data
Lincoln Park Zoo / Thomas Kingsley Troupe
Spooky Sites
ISBN 979-8-8904-2687-1 (hard cover)
ISBN 979-8-8904-2715-1 (paperback)
ISBN 979-8-8904-2743-4 (EPUB)
ISBN 979-8-8904-2771-7 (eBook)
Library of Congress Control Number: 2023922890

Printed in the United States of America.

Seahorse Publishing Company
seahorsepub.com

Copyright © 2025 **SEAHORSE PUBLISHING COMPANY**

All rights reserved. No part of this publication may be reproduced, stored in a retrieval system or be transmitted in any form or by any means, electronic, mechanical, photocopying, recording, or otherwise, without the prior written permission of Seahorse Publishing Company.

Published in the United States
Seahorse Publishing
PO Box 771325
Coral Springs, FL 33077